Rules For Happy Living

Children's Sermons And Activity Pages

Julia E. Bland

CSS Publishing Company, Inc., Lima, Ohio

Dedicated to
Sam, Andy, Paul, Mark, Mary, and Charles

Copyright © 1998 by
CSS Publishing Company, Inc.
Lima, Ohio

ISBN: 978-0-7880-0766-8

Table Of Contents

Suggestions From The Author

Study the sermon so that you can tell it in your own words using your own personality and with the needs of your local children in mind.

The sermon as given is to get you started. Be open to the Holy Spirit as he guides you to add your own personal observations.

If you need notes, make them small and tuck them inside your Bible at the page where you will be reading the Scripture.

Open the Bible and read from it. Children need to know that what you say really is from the Scriptures.

Ask questions and allow time for the children to answer. This will get them thinking and involved, but children can say unexpected things, so be ready to guide them back to the subject.

Before the worship hour, clip the activity sheet, a pencil, and crayons to a clipboard to be ready to hand to each child when the children's time is over.

As you pray and prepare, claim the Lord's promise in Isaiah 55:11:

So shall my word be that goes out from my mouth;
it shall not return to me empty,
but it shall accomplish that which I purpose,
and succeed in the thing for which I sent it.

Julia Bland

Rules For Happy Living

Jesus gave us rules for a happy life.

Scripture: Matthew 22:37-39; 7:12a

Visual Aid: A bat and ball.

Handouts: Activity sheets.

Advance Preparations: Make copies of the activity sheets, enough for each child to have one.

The Sermon:

Before you play a game, what do you have to know? The rules, of course. Do you like to play ball? *What are some of the rules for playing ball? Just suppose you and your friends choose up sides to play ball. One team takes the field. The other is up to bat. The first batter says, "I'm not going to be out until I have six strikes." The second batter says, "I'm staying up until I hit the ball." The third batter says, "I'm not making a fool of myself trying to hit the ball, I'm just running the bases." What would happen to such a game? Would the game be ruined? Would there even be a game? Would there be any winners? No. Everyone would be a loser.

Did you know there are rules, also, for living? Yes, and our lives are more than a game. If we don't live by the rules, life too will be ruined. If we do live by the rules, we are sure to be a winner! Jesus gave us the rules. There are two. He calls them commandments. They are found in the Bible. Listen carefully to Matthew 22:37-39:

> *He said to him* (and to us), *"You shall love the Lord your God with all your heart, and with all your soul, and with all your mind. This is the greatest and first commandment. And a second is like it: You shall love your neighbor as yourself."*

We cannot make up our own rules. We are not wise enough. So we must listen to Jesus. What are the rules? The first one is that we must love God with all our hearts. The second one is that we must love others. Jesus helps us understand that second one better when he says in Matthew 7:12:

> *"In everything do to others as you would have them do to you ..."*

We'll be talking about Jesus' two rules another day.

*Use visual aids

The Two Greatest Commandments: The Love Laws

Everything we need to know from the Old Testament is in the two commandments of Jesus.

Scripture: Matthew 22:35-40

Visual Aid: Bible with the Old Testament, the picture of the scroll from the activity sheet, colored with crayons or markers.

Handouts: Activity sheets.

Advance Preparations: Make copies of the activity sheets, enough for each child to have one. Make an extra copy of side one (the scroll) and color it. Have it ready for use during the sermon time.

The Sermon:

Do you know what a law is? A law is a rule telling us how to act or perhaps how to behave. It tells us what must be done or not done or perhaps how to do it. For instance, we have traffic laws or rules. Can you think of any? Why do we have traffic laws? Do they protect us?

When Jesus lived, his people had a lot of laws in their religion. Some were laws about what they could or could not eat, what kinds of dishes to use, and how to wash. They were especially careful about how to keep the Sabbath day holy. Some people thought the most important thing in their life was the careful keeping of these laws. They thought this pleased God. One day one of these law keepers wanted to see what Jesus knew and believed about the laws, so he asked him a question. We read this in Matthew 22:35-40:

> *... a lawyer asked him a question to test him. "Teacher, which commandment in the law is the greatest?" He said to him, "You shall love the Lord your God with all your heart, and with all your soul, and with all your mind. This is the greatest and first commandment. And a second is like it: You shall love your neighbor as yourself. On these two commandments hang all the law and the prophets."*

What did he ask? What did Jesus tell him?

But Jesus knew exactly what they all needed to hear. Jesus knew that they were so busy trying to keep all their laws that they had no time for what was really important; they had no time for love. So Jesus gave them his two laws, laws of love. And what is more, he told them that all of the Scripture that they had and were so proud of was based on or came from those two laws of love. Verses 40 says:

> *"On these two commandments hang all the law and the prophets."*

The Law and the prophets that Jesus was talking about are found here in the Old Testament* part of our Bible. In Jesus' time, scripture was written not in a book like ours but in scrolls something like our color picture on our activity sheet.* Jesus said all of this* was written to explain and help us understand these two short laws. What are the two laws?

1. We must love the Lord our God with all our hearts, souls, and minds.
2. We must love others as we love ourselves.

The two laws must be very important. Jesus thought so. He means for us to keep these love laws. How can you show your love for God? What are some ways you can love others?

*Use visual aids

Loving Jesus, God's Messenger

We show our love for God by loving his Son, whom he sent.

Scripture: John 6:28-29; 5:24

Visual Aid: Magazine or newspaper ads with a message.

Handouts: Activity sheets.

Advance Preparations: Make copies of the activity sheet, enough for each child to have one.

The Sermon:

Do you know what a message is? It's something someone needs or wants to tell. *Here are some messages in this magazine (newspaper). We'll read one. This was a written message. Some written messages are found on signs along the highway, but people can carry messages too. Let's suppose that you are outside playing and Mom sends your brother or sister out to find you with a message. The message is "Come in now, it's time for supper." What will you do? Would you believe Mom really sent your brother or sister? Suppose you didn't believe it. Suppose you didn't go in? Would you get in trouble? Would you miss your supper? Suppose you said, "I don't believe Mom sent you. I don't believe there is any supper," or "I'll think about it and maybe I'll come tomorrow." You wouldn't do that, would you?

Yet sometimes people treat Jesus that way. They don't believe Jesus was God's son and that he came from God with a message. Or worse yet, some people ignore him. In John 6:28 some people asked Jesus, "What does God want us to do?" And so in verse 29:

> *Jesus answered them, "This is the work of God, that you believe in him whom he has sent."*
> (meaning himself)

If we are going to love God with all our hearts, as Jesus has said in his first rule, then we must do as God wishes and believe that Jesus was God's son and came from God with a message. What is that message? It is that God wants to be our father, that God loves us, that God cares, that he wants to forgive, and that he wants us to have a happy life now and life eternal with him someday. Jesus proved this message from God was true when he died for us on the cross. Whoever believes Jesus and the message he brought from God has eternal life. We read this promise in John 5:24:

> *"Very truly, I tell you, anyone who hears my word* (message) *and believes him who sent me has eternal life...."*

Let's believe Jesus and his message! Let's love him for coming from God. Let's ask him to be our own Lord and Savior!

*Use visual aids

Loving God

We show our love for God in obedience and in worship.

Scripture: Colossians 3:16; Matthew 18:19-20; John 14:15; 15:12

Visual Aid: Church furniture: the altar, the pulpit, the piano, and so forth.

Handouts: Activity sheets.

Advance Preparations: Make copies of the activity sheet, enough for each child to have one.

The Sermon:

What did Jesus say was the most important of all commands or rules? That we must love the Lord with all our hearts, with all our souls and with all our minds. How can we do this? How do we show our love for him? First of all, Jesus said in John 14:15, "If you love me you will keep my commandments." And in John 15:12, he says, "This is my commandment, that you love one another as I have loved you."

Jesus is saying we show our love for him when we obey his command to love each other. But there is another way to show our love for the Lord, and that is by our worship. What do we mean by worship? Worship is honoring the Lord. We do this by our prayers, our thanksgiving, our songs, our reading the Bible, and by hearing God's word taught and preached. We do these things in church, don't we? The Bible tells us in Colossians 3:16:

> *Let the word of Christ dwell in you richly; teach and admonish one another in all wisdom; and with gratitude in your hearts sing psalms, hymns, and spiritual songs to God.*

The church building and furniture are made to help us. *See the altar; it's a place to kneel for prayer. Some people take communion at the altar. Our church also has a pulpit where God's word from the Bible is preached. We have a piano (perhaps an organ) to help us in our worship with music. We could worship God other places with prayer, songs, and Bible reading, and we should daily, but coming to church with our friends helps our worship. God knew this and he planned for us to worship together so that we could be encouraged by one another. Then, too, Jesus promised a special blessing when we gather. He promised his own presence and answer to our prayers. Listen to Matthew 18:19-20:

> *"Again, truly I tell you, if two of you agree on earth about anything you ask, it will be done for you by my Father in heaven. For where two or three are gathered in my name, I am there among them."*

Isn't it wonderful to think that Jesus is present with us here, now? No, we don't see him, but his spirit is here.

*Use visual aids

Jesus Commands Us To Love

Love is for God; love is for people.

Scripture: John 15:12

Visual Aid: A turnip or other unpopular vegetable; chocolate chip cookies.

Handouts: Activity sheets; cookies.

Advance Preparations: Make copies of the activity sheets, enough for each child to have one.

The Sermon:

Do you remember what Jesus said were the two most important laws of all? First, we should love God, not just a little, but with all our hearts, our souls, and our minds. Second, that we should love each other, not just a little, but as much as we love ourselves.

Sometimes we use the word "love" carelessly. *Do you say you love turnips? Probably not, even though vegetables are very good for us, often we don't love them. *But, you might say you love chocolate chip cookies! Do we really love them? Love is for something more important than a cookie. Jesus said in John 15:12:

> *"This is my commandment, that you love one another as I have loved you."*

Jesus didn't say, "Wouldn't it be nice if my people love each other." He said, "I command you to love." Does Mom or Dad say, "Wouldn't it be nice if you went to bed now?" No, they say, "Do it." It's a command and they expect you to obey. Jesus expects us to love. It is a command that we must try to obey. Some people are very hard to love. They are cross or rude, or they hurt us. Praying for them helps us to love them. But love doesn't mean that we need to be with these people all the time, nor that we must have them for best friends. It doesn't mean we have to want to hug and kiss. Love is caring and being concerned that others are all right, inside where their feelings are and outside where their need of food, clothing, and shelter is. It is a concern that they, too, know about Jesus and his love. We can even love someone we don't know by caring that everything is all right with them. This is what we are doing when we give to help people who have had trouble, such as a flood or an earthquake. Or when you give so that missionaries can go tell people who we don't know about Jesus. We are loving. We love, because Jesus commands it.

*Use visual aids

We Know What's Important

People are more important than things.

Scripture: Matthew 12:9-14; 7:12a

Visual Aid: VIP badges; a picture of a bus, if available.

Handouts: Activity sheets; a VIP badge for everyone.

Advance Preparations: Use the VIP badge from the activity sheet as a pattern and make enough for each child, color and have them ready to pin on. Make copies of the activity sheets.

The Sermon:

Do you know what a VIP is? *A VIP is a "very important person." Maybe you think a very important person is a king or queen or the President of the United States. Let's see if that is so. I want to tell you a true story. One time at a certain place in England it was decided that *buses would no longer stop to pick up passengers. They said that if they stopped to pick up passengers it would disrupt their schedules. This seems funny at first, but maybe it's not. What kind of bus service is it that doesn't consider the needs of people? They were mixed up on what's important. What do you think is most important, the people that need the ride or the bus time schedule?

There were mixed-up people when Jesus lived, too. The religious people thought nothing was more important than keeping their rule about the Sabbath day. The rule was that no one could do any work on that day. In Matthew 12 the Bible tells us that one Sabbath day Jesus found a man with a crippled hand and healed him. Healing on the Sabbath day was work, the religious people said, and it made them very angry that Jesus had broken their rule. They were not thinking about the poor man with the crippled hand, only about their rule. Jesus said to them:

> *"Suppose one of you has only one sheep and it falls into a pit on the sabbath; will you not lay hold of it and lift it out? How much more valuable is a human being than a sheep! So it is lawful to do good on the sabbath."* — Matthew 12:11-12

Were these people mixed up on what's important? Yes. They were even more willing to help a sheep than a person in need. Jesus scolded them for this attitude. Sometimes we get mixed up on what's important. At home we might worry about our stuff or a clean house more than the feelings and comfort of others. In our church, do we worry about a dirty carpet, or are we just glad that the feet of people have brought them to worship? Or in the church kitchen, do we fuss about dirty glasses, or are we glad someone came, got thirsty, and had a drink? Do you remember the golden rule? Can we say it together? This rule helps us to remember that just as we want our needs to be important, so must we be concerned about the needs of others. Jesus never, never got mixed up: to him people were more important than anything! To him everyone is a VIP! *And that is just what each of you are, a Very Important Person.

*Use visual aids

The Greatest Old Master

We accept all people the way God has made them.

Scripture: Genesis 1:27, 31; Matthew 7:12a

Visual Aid: A print of a painting by an old master.

Handouts: Activity sheets.

Advance Preparations: Make copies of the activity sheets. Your local church may have a picture of the *Last Supper* by Leonardo da Vinci for the children to see. If not, look in the library in the art appreciation section. The librarian will help find something suitable to show the children. Be ready to tell a sentence or two about the painting and the artist.

The Sermon:

Do you know what an old master is? An old master was an artist who lived several hundred years ago. The art they created was so good it is still being admired and copied. Maybe you've seen a copy of the painting called the *Last Supper* with Jesus and his disciples painted by Leonardo di Vinci. Or perhaps you've heard of Michelangelo, who was a sculptor, painter, and architect. *I brought this one to show.... The art works of old masters are treasured in art museums around the world. Have you ever visited an art museum? I hope everyone will sometime.

But who do you think was the greatest old master of all? God, of course. What was his masterpiece? He made many, but I'm thinking of the one he especially loves and died for. Let's read from Genesis 1:27:

So God created humankind in his image, in the image of God he created them; male and female he created them.

God made people sort of like himself. And the Bible says that God likes his masterpiece. Verse 31 says:

God saw everything that he had made, and indeed, it was very good.

God made everyone the way they are, something like himself. So then we must accept others the way God has made them. We never, never make fun of the way anyone looks, even if we think they look different or are too fat, too thin, too tall, or too short. What does our Golden Rule say? We accept others the way God has made them, just as we want them to accept us. God does. They, just like you, are God's masterpiece.

*Use visual aids

We Include All

We watch for a chance to include everyone.

Scripture: Matthew 7:12a; Galatians 6:10

Visual Aid: Paper dolls cut in a circle.

Handouts: Activity sheets; paper dolls.

Advance Preparation: Make copies of the activity sheets; practice making the circle of paper dolls, following the instructions on the activity sheet. Have one folded, drawn, and ready to cut. Each of the children would enjoy having one to unfold too. These should be folded and cut out in advance.

The Sermon:
What were the two great rules or commandments that Jesus gave? We are to love God and each other. God's people are to look for things that need doing. Let's hear what Jesus said in Matthew 7:12. See if you hear the word "do."

"In everything DO to others what you would have them do to you."

Have you ever cut out paper dolls? *After you fold exactly right, you cut, making sure not to cut across the folds at the hands and feet. If you do cut the folds, they'll fall apart. Now I have one ready, and here is one for each of you. Let's unfold them together. Look! Everyone is in a circle. None is left out. This is the way it should be. How would you feel if you got left out of games others are playing? Be sure to include others when you play. How would you feel if everyone had enough to eat and wear, a place to sleep, and necessary medicine, but you didn't? How would you feel if everyone but you knew about Jesus and his love? I would feel very bad. I know you would, too. So God's people watch for the chance to give, to share, to include all. Listen to what the Bible says in Galatians 6:10:

So then, whenever we have an opportunity, let us work for the good of all, and especially for those of the family of faith.

This tells us we work for the good of all. No one gets left out.

*Use visual aids

Care And Bear

God's people look for things that need doing.

Scripture: Matthew 7:12a; Galatians 6:2

Visual Aid: A dish rag and a dish towel.

Handouts: Activity sheets.

Advance Preparation: Make copies of the activity sheets.

The Sermon:

Does anyone remember the Golden Rule? Can you say it? Let's read it from the Bible:

"In everything do to others as you would have them do to you."

Who said this? It was Jesus. We might say, "Well, I won't have any trouble with that because I don't quarrel or fight nor am I unkind. Good. But the Golden Rule is more than "don'ts." It is also "do." "Do" is an action word. God's people look for things that need doing. Today we are talking about two words. The two words are "care" and "bear." God's people should be caring, wanting everything to be all right for others. Are we selfish and only care about what we want, think, or are? Do we really have thought for what others want and need? Just suppose Mom says her head hurts and asks us to please turn off the television. Do we get mad? stomp? pout? slam doors? Even grown-ups can do this when they don't get their way. We need to care.

What about the word "bear"? "Bear" means we do more than care. Let's see what the Bible says:

Bear one another's burdens, and in this way you will fulfill the law of Christ.

This is saying that not only should we care, we should also bear or help. Now, suppose you turn off the television gladly because you care for Mom. Then you offer to help, pick up your room, or do some chores. This is bearing Mom's burden as the Bible says we should.

*Do you know what a dish rag and a dish towel are for? Do you know how to use them? Do you know that a table has to be cleared off after eating? Perhaps the crumbs swept up? You can help Mom even if her head doesn't hurt! What are other ways you can help Mom or Dad? All God's people should care and bear.

*Use visual aids

Why We Share

We share cheerfully because sharing brings happiness to ourselves, to others, and to God.

Scripture: Acts 20:35b; 2 Corinthians 9:7b

Visual Aid: Gum or wrapped treats, enough for each child to have two, one to keep and one to share.

Handouts: Activity sheets.

Advance Preparations: Make copies of the activity sheets, enough for each child to have one.

The Sermon:

Have you ever heard these words, "You must share"? When tiny children play together, mothers and dads say this a lot. How about you, has anyone ever said, "You must share," to you? Do you want to? Is it hard? Sometimes it is. *I brought some gum for myself. After church I'm going to chew it. Shall I keep it and chew it all? Of course, I won't. Here are two for each of you. One is for you and one is for you to share with someone.

Sharing is not just Mom or Dad's idea. God also says we must share. Why? There are some very good reasons. One is we make others happy. Also we make ourselves happy. Listen to what the Bible says in Acts 20:35:

> ... the Lord Jesus ... himself said, "It is more blessed to give than to receive."

The word "blessed" means happiness. In other words, it is a happy thing to give. Sharing makes God happy, too, if we share willingly and cheerfully. Listen to this from 2 Corinthians 9:7b:

> ... God loves a cheerful giver.

Another reason we share is because we like others to share with us. When we do, we are obeying the rule Jesus gave to us. We must do to others what we want them to do to us.

*Use visual aids

Scoring

We forgive because we need to be forgiven.

Scripture: Matthew 18:21-22

Visual Aid: Newspaper sports page that gives scores.

Handouts: Activity sheets.

Advance Preparation: Make copies of the activity sheets.

The Sermon:

How can we tell who has won when teams play games? Is it by keeping score? The scores for such games as football, basketball, baseball, and softball are given in the newspaper.* The players might be on school teams, college teams, or professional teams. If you are interested in a certain team, you like to know if they won and what the score was. *Let's read a score or two here. A team wins by scoring the most. In baseball, all kinds of scores are kept, such as how many times a batter hits the ball, how many times a batter strikes out, how many times a player steals a base, how many errors a player makes, how many men a player puts out, how many men the pitcher strikes out, how many balls the pitcher throws, or how many home runs the pitcher allows. There seems to be no end to the scores kept for each player. Of course, the most important score is the team score and which team won. Keeping score in games is fun.

BUT there is another kind of keeping score that is not good and does not please Jesus. It goes like this: how many times does someone, perhaps brother or sister, get something and you don't, or how much work you did and they didn't. Perhaps we remember exactly how many times someone has lost his or her temper and hurt our feelings. Do you think Jesus likes us to keep this kind of score? In the Bible we read that Peter wanted to keep score, too:

> *Then Peter came and said to him, "Lord, if another member of the church sins against me, how often should I forgive? As many as seven times?" Jesus said to him, "Not seven times, but, I tell you, seventy times seven."* — Matthew 18:21-22

If someone did something against him, Peter thought a score of seven times of forgiving was enough. But Jesus said seventy times seven. How many is that? It's 490. Could you keep a score of forgiving against someone who did wrong 490 times? Probably not. We'd lose track, we'd forget, and we'd be in such a habit of forgiving by that time that we wouldn't want to keep score. What Jesus probably meant was that we should never keep this kind of score. We should always be forgiving. We forgive others, just as we want to be forgiven. This is following Jesus' rule of loving others. We do to others what we want them to do to us: we forgive. There is another thing we need to remember. Jesus also said that if we want him to forgive us when we've done wrong, then we **must** forgive others. This is not easy but this is what Jesus expects, and if we'll really try, then he will help.

*Use visual aids

Jesus, Lord Of Our Hearts

If Jesus is Lord, we'll obey his commands.

Scripture: Matthew 22:37-39; Romans 10:9

Visual Aid: A heart with a folded-back hole.

Handouts: Activity sheets.

Advance Preparation: Copy the activity sheets, one for each child. Make an extra copy of the heart from the activity sheet, cut out, color the figure of Jesus with crayons or markers. Cut along the top, left side and bottom lines. Do not cut the right side line. Use it to fold the figure of Jesus back to make a hole in the heart. If you wish a sturdier heart, glue to construction paper before cutting.

The Sermon:

*I have here a heart. But something is wrong; something is missing. What's missing? Look! I'll fold this forward and see, it is the part that has **Jesus is Lord**. Jesus has given us two rules or commands for living a happy life. Remember them? Here they are again from Matthew 22:

> *"You shall love the Lord your God with all your heart, and with all your soul, and with all your mind. You shall love your neighbor as yourself."*

Why are some people so unhappy, doing unhappy things, even terrible, sinful things? Why do some people hate instead of love? It's because they don't know or keep Jesus' first rule. Like the paper heart,* Jesus and love for him is missing. That explains what's wrong with them. If Jesus were there and was Lord of their hearts they would love. What does it mean to have Jesus in our hearts? When we say heart here, we are not talking about the muscle in our bodies that pumps the blood and keeps us alive. What we are talking about is the place inside us that has deep feelings such as love or hate, anger or kindness, jealousy or compassion. So if Jesus is Lord of our hearts, he has become so important to us that he is as much a part of our lives as the real hearts that pump our blood through our bodies and keep us alive. Everything we do or say we try to please him because he is Lord of our hearts. To make him Lord, we must believe that he is truly God's son, that he died on the cross, and that he didn't stay dead but came alive again, all for us. But Jesus doesn't become part of our lives unless we want him and say so. Romans 10:9 tells us:

> *... if you confess with your lips that **Jesus is Lord** and believe in your heart that God raised him from the dead, you will be saved.*

Making Jesus Lord of our hearts, our souls, our minds, our whole lives saves us *from* the unhappy life that doesn't love, and that does sinful, hurting things. And Jesus saves us *to* a happy life of love and obedience with him now and forever. When Jesus is Lord of our hearts we can keep his two rules. We'll love God and we'll learn to love others.

*Use visual aids

He said to him, "You shall love the Lord your God with all your heart, and with all your soul, and with all your mind. This is the greatest and first commandment. And a second is like it: you shall love your neighbor as yourself."

— Matthew 22:37-39

RULES FOR HAPPY LIVING

JESUS SAID THIS:

"In everything do to others as you would have them do to you...."
— Matthew 7:12

We call it the **GOLDEN RULE**.

CROSS OUT THE SENTENCES THAT ARE NOT TRUE.

A game has rules.

Each person can make up his or her own rules.

We like to win.

A game is ruined if no one plays by the rules.

Jesus gave two great rules or commands.

Life can be ruined if we don't keep the rules Jesus gave.

Jesus' two rules are: love the Lord your God and love your neighbor as yourself.

If we love others, we will do to them what we would like them to do to us.

HELP FIND THE BALL.

DRAW A LINE TO THE WORDS THAT FINISH THE SENTENCE. ONE HAS BEEN DONE.

One side •
The other side •
The catcher •
The pitcher •
The batter tries •
Three strikes •
The batter that hits the ball •
The fielders try •
The batters score •
The greatest commandment is •
The second greatest commandment is •

• and you're out.
• is behind home plate.
• love the Lord your God.
• runs to first base.
• to put the batter out.
• is up to bat.
• is in the field.
• love your neighbor as yourself.
• to hit the ball.
• throws the ball across home plate.
• if they run the bases safely.

HE SAID TO HIM, "YOU SHALL LOVE THE LORD YOUR GOD WITH ALL YOUR HEART, AND WITH ALL YOUR SOUL, AND WITH ALL YOUR MIND. YOU SHALL LOVE YOUR NEIGHBOR AS YOURSELF. ON THESE TWO COMMANDMENTS HANG ALL THE LAW AND THE PROPHETS."
— MATTHEW 22:37, 39, 40

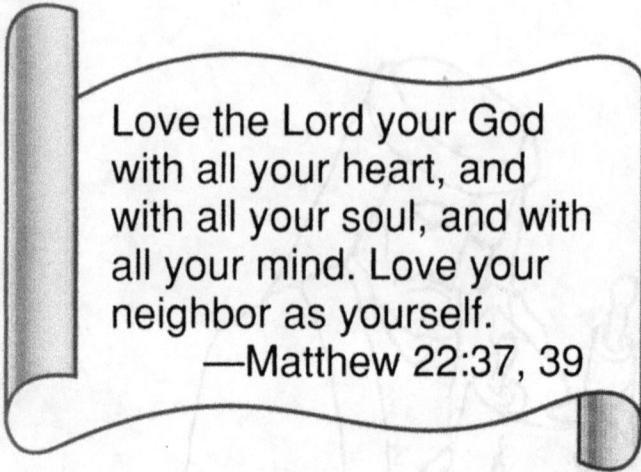

Love the Lord your God with all your heart, and with all your soul, and with all your mind. Love your neighbor as yourself.
—Matthew 22:37, 39

oevl   _ _ _ _

roLd   _ _ _ _

lla   _ _ _

arthe   _ _ _ _ _

uols   _ _ _ _

ndim   _ _ _ _

iehgnobr   _ _ _ _ _ _ _ _

selfruoy   _ _ _ _ _ _ _ _

FILL IN THE SQUARES WITH THE CORRECT WORDS.

L ___ ___ ___

DOWN
The two rules are called _____.

ACROSS
Jesus' two rules are about _____.

DOWN
First we must love _____.

___ ___ ___ R S

ACROSS
We also must love _____.

love
washing
eating
scripture
law
days
teaching
prophets
two
drinking

FILL IN THE BLANK FROM THE WORD LIST.

Jesus said the t_____ of the l_____ and p_____ of our Old Testament s_____ depends on t_____ laws or rules. These are not laws or rules about e_____ and d_____ and w_____ or keeping the d_____ holy. They are laws about l_____.

IF YOU DO DOT TO DOT IN THE FOUR BOXES, YOU WILL SPELL A WORD.

VERY TRULY, I TELL YOU, ANYONE WHO HEARS MY WORD AND BELIEVES HIM WHO SENT ME HAS ETERNAL LIFE....

— JOHN 5:24

LOVING JESUS, GOD'S MESSENGER

USE THE CODE IN THE BOX TO FIND ONE OF THE MESSAGES OF JESUS.

1=a	10=n
2=b	11=o
3=d	12=r
4=e	13=s
5=g	14=t
6=h	15=u
7=i	16=v
8=l	17=w
9=m	18=y

V E R Y T R U L Y I
16 4 12 18 14 12 15 8 18

T E L L you, A N Y O N E who
14 4 8 8 _____ 1 10 18 11 10 4

H E A R S my W O R D and
6 4 1 12 13 _____ 17 11 12 3

B E L I E V E S him who
2 4 8 7 4 16 4 13

S E N T me has E T E R N A L life....
13 4 10 14 _____ 4 14 4 12 10 1 8

— John 5:24

DO YOU KNOW HOW TO TAKE A MESSAGE FROM SOMEONE ON THE TELEPHONE? IF YOU DON'T KNOW, ASK MOM OR DAD TO TELL YOU.

UNDERLINE THE KIND OF MESSAGE BELOW THAT MIGHT COME ON THE TELEPHONE.

- Dad called to say he'll be late coming home from work.
- Where's my other shoe?
- Grandma called to say they're coming for a visit.
- Bobby hit me.
- Uncle Dan called to say they have a new baby girl.
- Bill called to say he'd pick us up at 9:30 for Sunday school.
- It's not my turn to set the table.
- Mr. Smith called to say he's done with repairs on the bike.
- I don't want to get up yet.

WHERE DO WE FIND THE MESSAGES FROM GOD THAT JESUS BROUGHT TO US? ____ ____ ____ ____ ____

magazines? dictionary?
map? telephone directory?
Bible? newspaper?

COULD A MESSAGE BE IN THE MAILBOX? CAN YOU FIND THE WAY THERE?

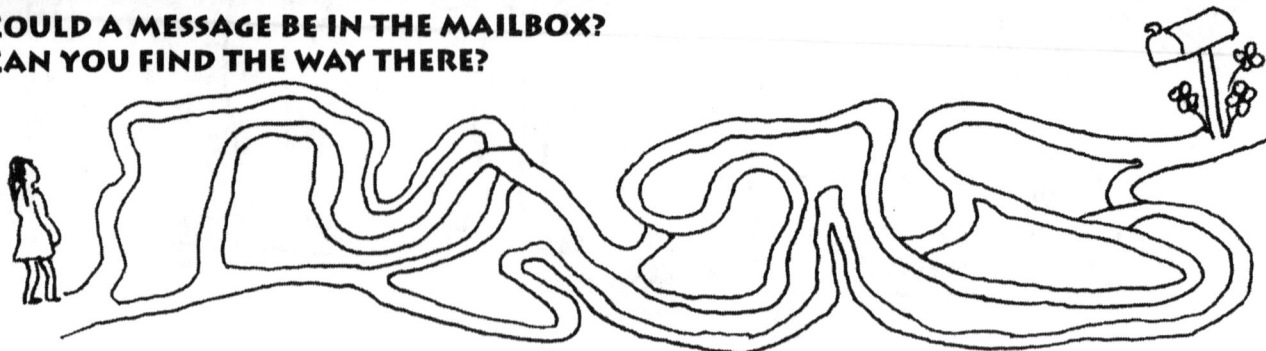

"FOR WHERE TWO OR THREE
ARE GATHERED IN MY NAME,
I AM THERE AMONG THEM."

— MATTHEW 18:20

LOVING GOD

SOME WORDS IN THIS VERSE MIGHT BE HARD TO UNDER-STAND. SEE IF YOU CAN FIGURE OUT THE CORRECT MEANING. DRAW A LINE TO WHAT YOU THINK THE WORD MEANS. WHEN YOU ARE DONE, CHECK YOUR ANSWERS AT THE BOTTOM OF THE PAGE.

Let the word of Christ dwell in you richly; teach and admonish one another in all wisdom; and with gratitude in your hearts sing psalms, hymns, and spiritual songs to God. — Colossians 3:16

1. word of Christ •	• 1. place of affections and deep feelings
2. dwell •	• 2. thankful for God's goodness
3. richly •	• 3. a sacred song from the Old Testament
4. teach •	• 4. as a precious possession
5. admonish •	• 5. understanding what is true and lasting
6. wisdom •	• 6. live
7. psalm •	• 7. gospel
8. hymns •	• 8. to help someone learn
9. spiritual •	• 9. to kindly warn
10. gratitude •	• 10. a song of praise or joy
11. hearts •	• 11. of or about God

CLIMB THE HILL TO CHURCH.

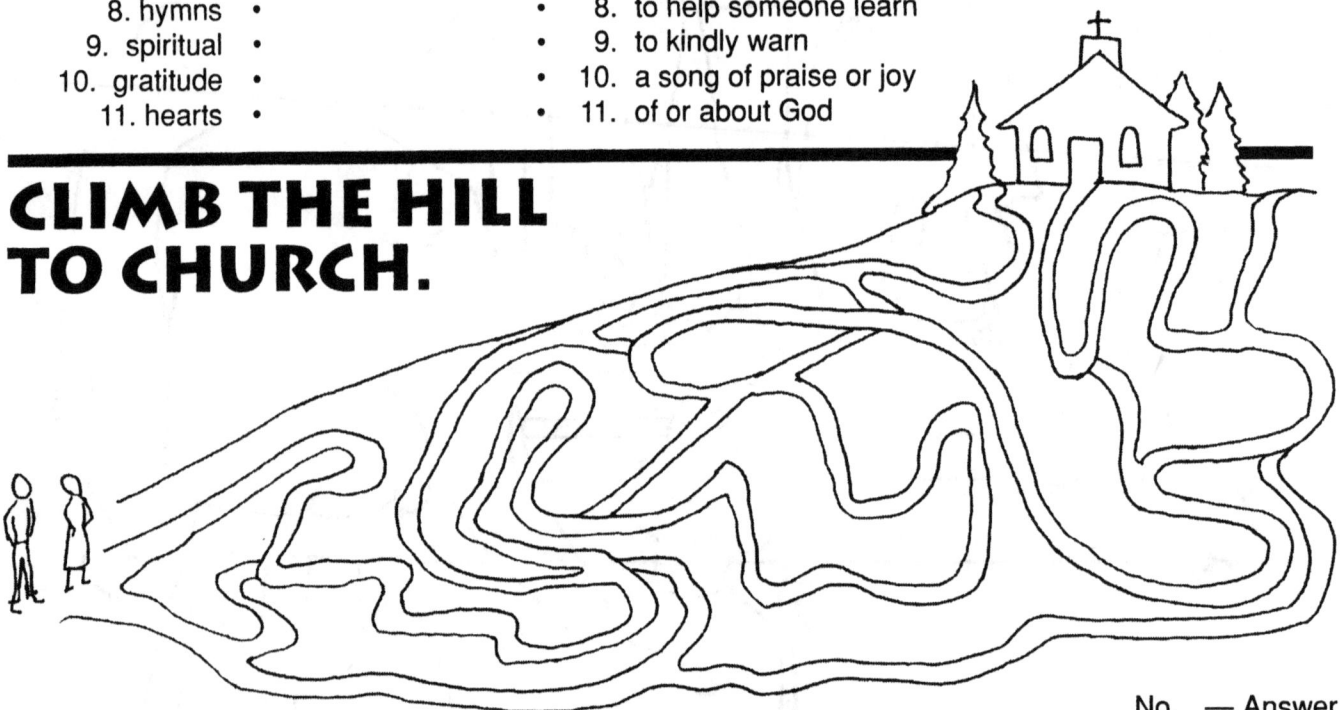

COMPLETE THE VERSE FROM THE WORD LIST BELOW.

FOR WHERE _ _ _ _ OR _ _ _ _ _ _ _ ARE _ _ _ _ _ _ _ _ _ _ _
IN MY _ _ _ _ _ _ AM THERE _ _ _ _ _ _ _ _ _ _ _ _.
— MATTHEW 18:20

gathered	among
I	three
them	name
two	

No.	—	Answer
1	—	7
2	—	6
3	—	4
4	—	8
5	—	9
6	—	5
7	—	3
8	—	10
9	—	11
10	—	2
11	—	1

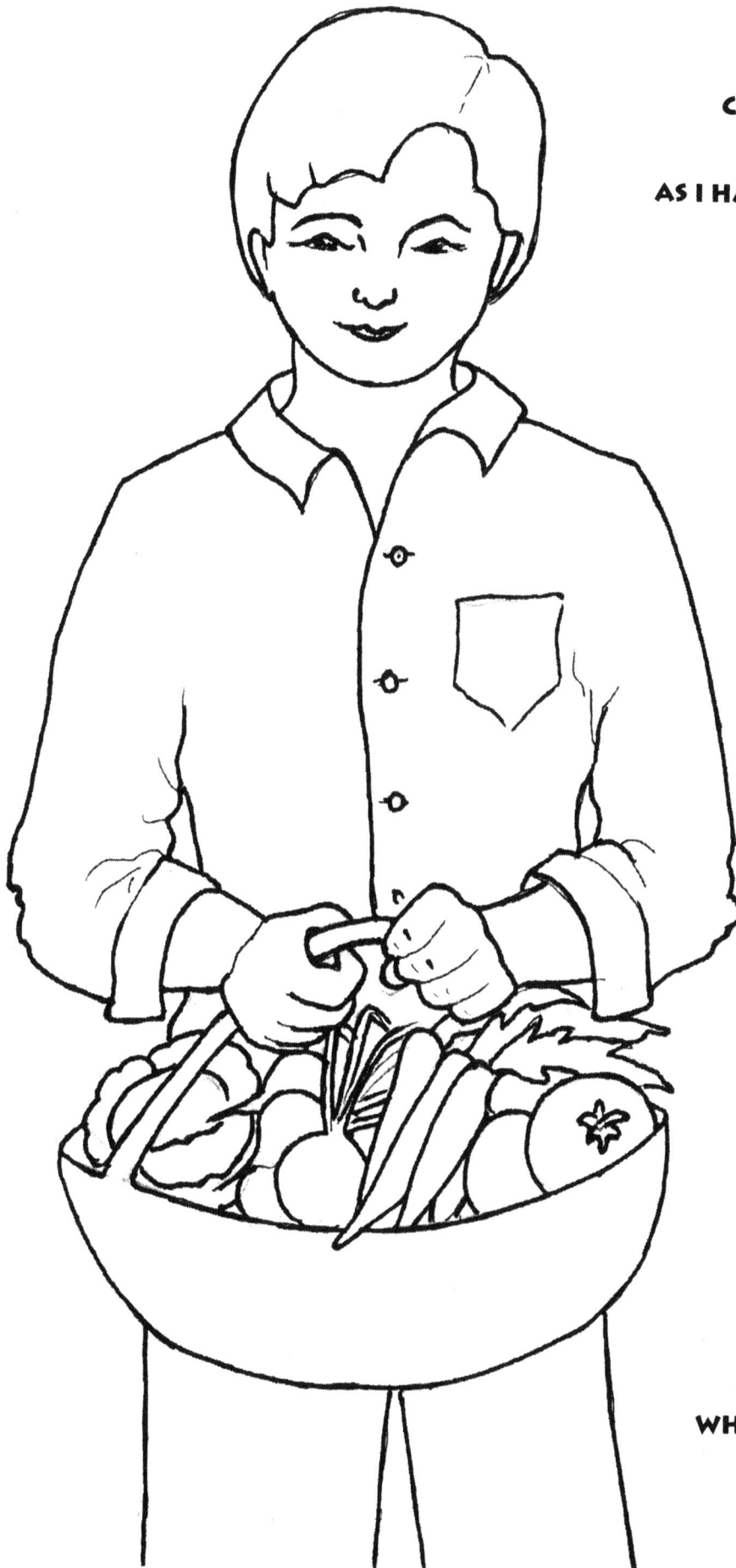

THIS IS MY
COMMANDMENT,
THAT YOU LOVE
ONE ANOTHER
AS I HAVE LOVED YOU.

—JOHN 15:12

TIM GIVES
VEGETABLES
TO NEIGHBORS
WHO HAVE NONE.

JESUS COMMANDS US TO LOVE

UNSCRAMBLE THE WORDS.

THIS IS MY _ _ _ _ _ _ _ _ _ _ _ _ , THAT YOU _ _ _ _ _ ONE ANOTHER
AS I _ _ _ _ _ LOVED _ _ _ . — JOHN 15:12

dmtencomman   ovle   aehv   uoy

FIND THE MISSING WORDS TO COMPLETE THE SENTENCE.

Jesus ☐☐☐☐☐ his people to love each other.

We must try to ☐☐☐ .

We can love by ☐☐☐☐☐☐ .

We want them to know about ☐☐☐☐☐ .

We want them to have what they ☐☐☐☐ .

We love others when we ☐☐☐☐ for them.

☐☐☐☐☐☐☐☐☐☐ are good for us but we don't love them.

Chocolate chip cookies ☐☐☐☐☐ very good but we don't love them.

☐☐☐☐ is for God.

Love is for ☐☐☐☐☐☐ .

Vegetables

expects

people

taste

Love

pray

obey

Jesus

caring

need

DRAW A LINE TO THE RIGHT VEGETABLE.

Some people put a slice raw on their hamburger.

A slice of this red one is good fresh.

This is good mashed with butter or gravy.

Eat this one cooked and right off the cob.

Cream these for a treat.

These are orange and good in soup.

This one makes good cole slaw.

This one is white with a purple top.

What is it? t _ _ _ _ _ p.

**WE ARE GLAD FOR ALL
THE GOOD THINGS
GOD CREATED FOR US TO ENJOY.**

"SUPPOSE ONE OF YOU HAS ONLY ONE SHEEP AND IT FALLS INTO A PIT ON THE SABBATH; WILL YOU NOT LAY HOLD OF IT AND LIFT IT OUT? HOW MUCH MORE VALUABLE IS A HUMAN BEING THAN A SHEEP! SO IT IS LAWFUL TO DO GOOD ON THE SABBATH." THEN HE SAID TO THE MAN, "STRETCH OUT YOUR HAND." HE STRETCHED IT OUT, AND IT WAS RESTORED, AS SOUND AS THE OTHER.
— MATTHEW 12:11-13

WE KNOW WHAT'S IMPORTANT

FINISH AND COLOR THE __ __ __.

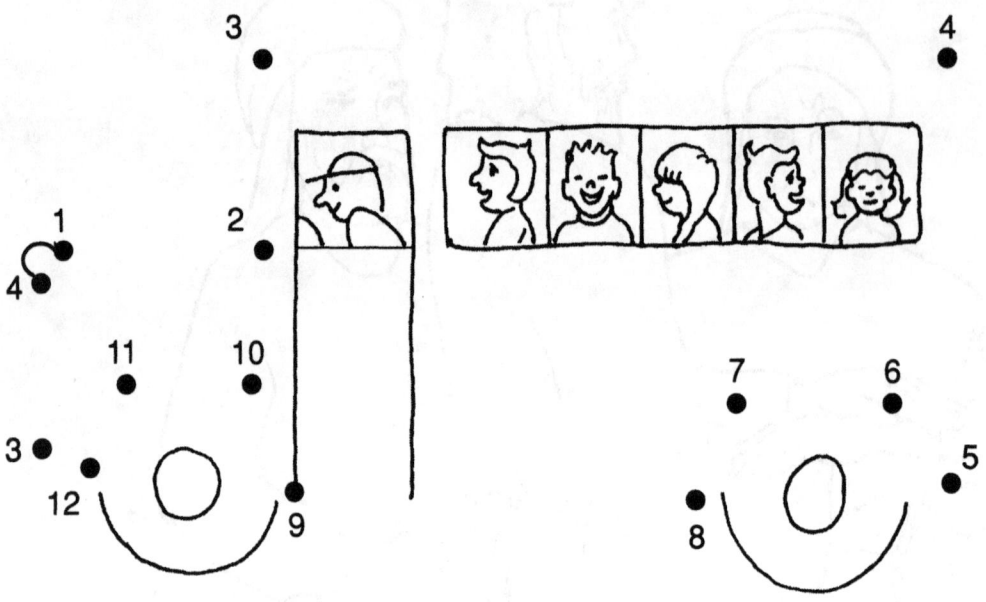

I KNOW THAT
I AM A VIP
BECAUSE JESUS LOVED
AND DIED FOR ME.

I KNOW THAT YOU
ARE A VIP, TOO,
BECAUSE JESUS LOVED
AND DIED FOR YOU.

3
4
1
2
4
11   10
7   6
3
12
9
5
8

BUSES ARE FOR PEOPLE

A BUS TAKES PEOPLE WHERE THEY NEED TO GO. CHOOSE WORDS FROM THE LIST TO FILL IN THE BOXES AND COMPLETE THE SENTENCE.

People might ride on a bus to

☐☐☐☐☐☐

or to

☐☐☐☐☐☐☐☐'☐   ☐☐☐☐☐

or to see a

☐☐☐☐☐☐.

England
school
the moon
doctor
fishing
grandma's house

Very Important Person

FILL IN THE MISSING LETTERS.

EVERYONE is a __ery __mportant __erson!

In Bible times sheep were very valuable. They were used for meat, milk, and clothing. The clothing was either wool or sheep skins. Oil came from sheep, and medicine bottles were made from their horns. A sheep horn was used to call people to worship. Sheep were used in sacrifices as offerings to God. When a poor family only had one, it was usually the family pet. But Jesus said a human being was more
__ __ __ __ __ __ __ __ than a sheep.

THE NEEDS OF ALL PEOPLE ARE IMPORTANT TO GOD AND TO GOD'S PEOPLE.

SO GOD CREATED HUMANKIND IN HIS IMAGE, IN THE IMAGE OF GOD HE CREATED THEM; MALE AND FEMALE HE CREATED THEM. GOD SAW EVERYTHING THAT HE HAD MADE, AND INDEED, IT WAS VERY GOOD.

— GENESIS 1:27, 31a

FRIENDS VISIT AN ART MUSEUM.

THE GREATEST OLD MASTER

m a s t e r p i e c e
x g h h x x e m x b a
x r o i x x o a m i n
x e r n x x p g a r i
f a t a l l l e s d m
i t x a c c e p t s a
s e n j o y x x e x l
h s g o o d h u r t s
o t h e r s v e r y x

WORDS TO LOOK FOR:

masterpiece	thin	image
greatest	accept	very
others	good	fish
fat	people	birds
tall	master	animals
short	hurt	enjoy

ALL WORDS GO LEFT TO RIGHT OR DOWN. CIRCLE THEM AND USE THEM TO FINISH THE SENTENCES BELOW.

Each of us is a _ _ _ _ _ _ _ _ _ _ _

made by God the _ _ _ _ _ _ _ _ _ old

_ _ _ _ _ _ of all. If we think someone is too

_ _ _ _ or _ _ _ _ _ or looks different,

remember God made all _ _ _ _ _ _ in his

own _ _ _ _ _. We _ _ _ _ _ _

everyone the way God has made them, just like

we want everyone to accept us. The Bible says

God saw all that he had made and it was

_ _ _ _ _ _ _ _ _. If we make fun of

_ _ _ _ _ _ _ we _ _ _ _ them and we

hurt God. God made many masterpieces,

_ _ _ _ _ for the sea, _ _ _ _ _ to fly

and all kinds of _ _ _ _ _ _ _. We

_ _ _ _ _ God's wonderful creation.

YOU WILL NEED A PENCIL AND AN ERASER TO DRAW THIS BIRD.

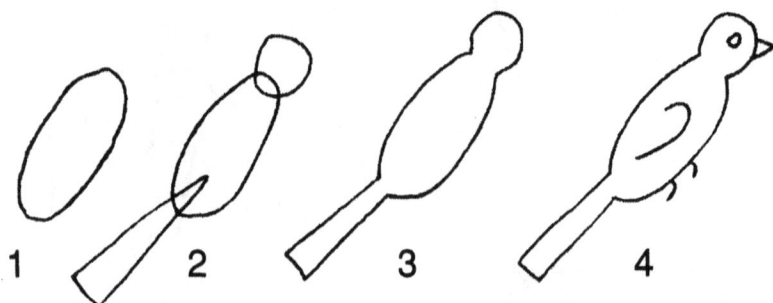

1   2   3   4

DRAW HERE

1. Draw an oval tipped to one side.
2. Draw a circle on the top end. Draw a long skinny triangle at the other end.
3. Erase the lines as shown.
4. Make a comma shape on the body for the wing. Draw a small triangle on the head for the beak. Make 2 small commas for feet. Add a small circle for the eye.

SO THEN, WHENEVER WE
HAVE AN OPPORTUNITY,
LET US WORK FOR THE GOOD
OF ALL, AND ESPECIALLY FOR
THOSE OF THE FAMILY OF FAITH.
— GALATIANS 6:10

31

PAPER DOLLS IN A CIRCLE

- Use a square piece of paper 8 inches or larger.
- Fold A to B and you have figure 1.
- Fold C to E to get the center line. Undo the fold, figure 1.
- Fold C to D and E to D and you have figure 2.
- Fold along dotted lines shown on figures 3 and 3b.
- Fold K and J backward and you have figure 4.
- Cut along the dotted line L M in figure 5.

There are sixteen layers folded together and each one makes a doll. Draw a doll on the top layer only, figure 6. Cut through all the layers with sharp scissors, figure 7. Do not cut through the ends of the arms or feet, because the dolls are held together at these places.

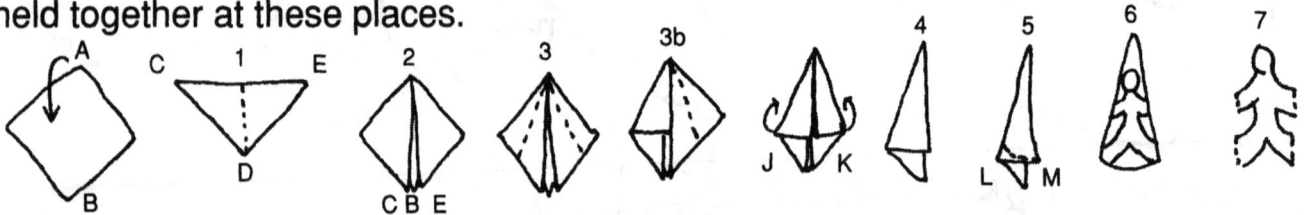

UNSCRAMBLE THE WORDS TO COMPLETE THE BIBLE VERSE.

So then, 1_____ we have an

2_____, let us 3_____

for the 4_____ of all, and especially for

5_____ of the 6_____ of

7_____ . 8_____ 6:10

THERE HAS BEEN A FLOOD.
HELP DELIVER WARM BLANKETS.

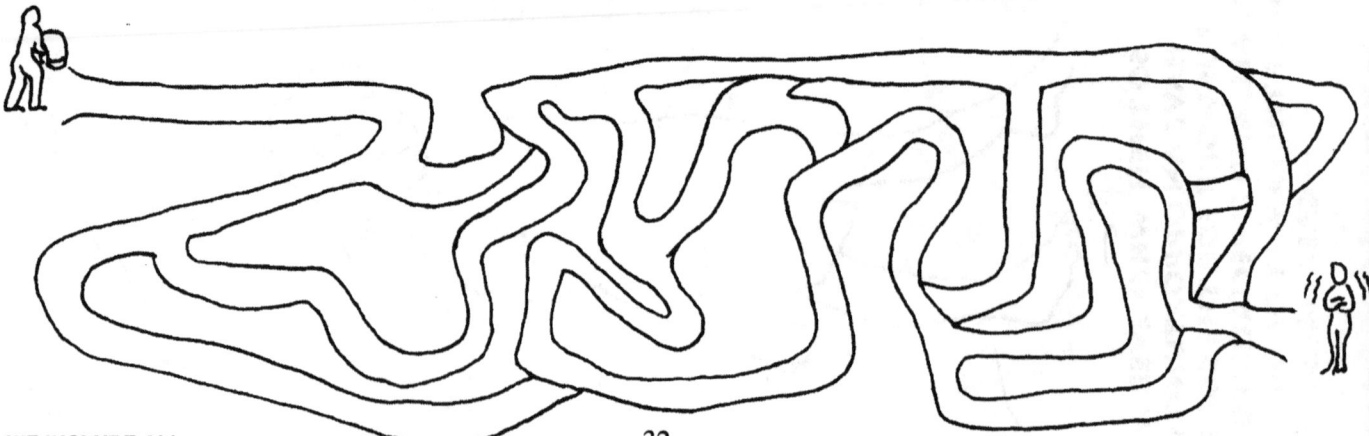

1. enhwvree
2. tunoppityor
3. krwo
4. oodg
5. oesht
6. mlyifa
7. iahtf
8. atGlaains

BILL AND JEAN HELP.

BEAR ONE ANOTHER'S BURDENS, AND IN THIS WAY YOU WILL FULFILL THE LAW OF CHRIST. — GALATIANS 6:2

CARE AND BEAR

```
a c e f u n t o g i k l
m o e v e r y t h i n g
f u l f i l l h a v e k
y x a l c a r e a d d c
a c w d b e a r x o w f
g b u r d e n s i n p r
```

care	others
bear	do
to	fulfill
have	law
everything	burdens

In _____ do ___ _____ what you

would _____ them __ __ to you.   — Matthew 12:7

_____ one another's _____ , and in this way you will

_____ the ___ of Christ.   — Galatians 6:2

One word is left. What is it? _____

We _____ about how
(rhymes with bear)
others feel.

We help _____ their
(rhymes with care)
burdens.

LIST SOME WAYS YOU CAN HELP YOUR MOM AND DAD OR PERHAPS YOUR GRANDPARENTS.

_____
_____
_____
_____
_____
_____

<u>DO</u> IS AN <u>ACTION</u> WORD. GOD'S PEOPLE LOOK FOR THINGS THAT NEED <u>DOING</u>.

... THE LORD JESUS ... HIMSELF SAID: "IT IS MORE BLESSED TO GIVE THAN TO RECEIVE."
                                                    — **ACTS 20:35b**

WHY WE SHARE

UNSCRAMBLE THE WORDS TO MAKE A SENTENCE THAT MOMS AND DADS SAY OFTEN.

ouY ustm aresh

_ _ _ _ _ _ _ _ _ _ _ _ _ _ .

FILL IN THE BLANKS USING THE RIGHT WORD FROM THE LIST.

God wants us to _ _ _ _ _ _ .

When we share we make others _ _ _ _ _ _ .

Jesus said it is more blessed to _ _ _ _ _ than to receive.

We make _ _ _ _ _ _ _ _ _ _ happy when we share.

God wants us to share _ _ _ _ _ _ _ _ _ _ _ _ .

If we share we are obeying God's _ _ _ _ to do to others
as we want them to do to us.

give
happy
ourselves
cheerfully
share
rule

o	s	y	o	u	■	w	g	w	■
b	a	m	u	s	t	h	i	a	p
e	i	d	r	■	■	y	v	n	l
y	d	o	s	h	a	r	e	t	a
c	h	e	e	r	f	u	l	l	y
a	a	g	l	■	g	l	h	o	t
c	p	i	v	l	o	e	e	v	o
t	p	v	e	a	o	■	a	e	o
s	y	e	s	w	d	■	r	u	s

CIRCLE WORDS IN THE BOX THAT ARE IN THE LIST. THE WORDS GO ACROSS TO THE RIGHT OR DOWN.

ACROSS	DOWN	
you	ourselves	obey
must	give (2)	play
share	happy	Acts
cheerfully	rule	hear
	do	why
	love	said
	us	too
	law	want
	good	

READ THE PHRASES. IF THE PHRASE TELLS SOMETHING NICE TO SHARE, DRAW A LINE FROM THE PHRASE TO THE SUCKER. THE ONE HAS BEEN DONE TO SHOW YOU HOW. HOW MANY LINES DID YOU DRAW?

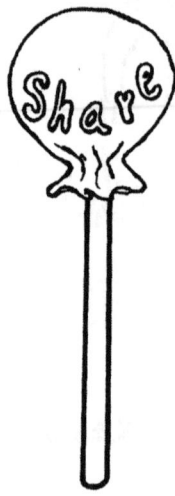

a bad cold

suckers

chickenpox

cookies

a turn on the swing

a piggyback ride with Dad

the front seat of the car

an argument

holding the kitten

a ride in the grocery cart

mud from your feet

batting the ball

crayons

fleas

THEN PETER CAME AND SAID TO HIM, "LORD, IF ANOTHER MEMBER OF THE CHURCH SINS AGAINST ME, HOW OFTEN SHOULD I FORGIVE? AS MANY AS SEVEN TIMES?" JESUS SAID TO HIM, "NOT SEVEN TIMES, BUT, I TELL YOU, SEVENTY TIMES SEVEN."

— MATTHEW 18:21-22

70 x 7 = 490

SCORING

_ _ _ _ _ _ had a question for Jesus.
Peter wanted to know how many times he
should _ _ _ _ _ _ _ someone.
Peter thought a _ _ _ _ _ _ of seven
times was enough.
Jesus said, "No, not _ _ _ _ _ times."
Jesus _ _ _ _ _ _ _ _, "Forgive
seventy times seven."
Seventy _ _ _ _ _ seven is 490.

USE THESE WORDS TO COMPLETE THE SENTENCES.

times
seven
forgive
Peter
answered
score

DOWN
Jesus said we must _ _ _ _ _ _ _ _ _.

ACROSS
The only way we should keep _ _ _ _ _ _
  is in fun.

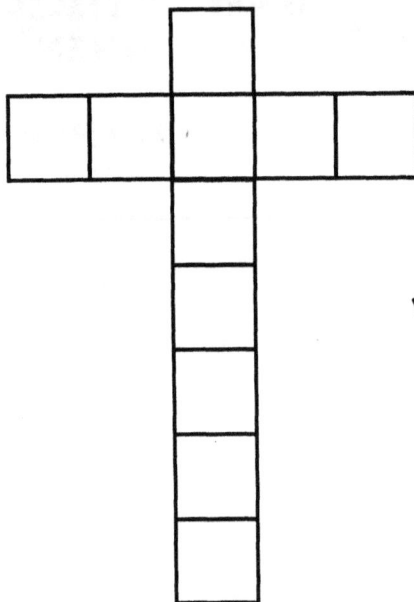

WHAT KIND OF BALL IS THIS?

_ _ _ _ _ _ _ ball

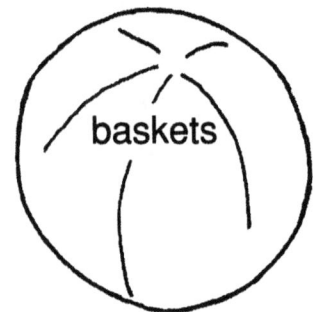

baskets

runs

_ _ _ _ _ ball

Scoring

_ _ _ _ _ ball

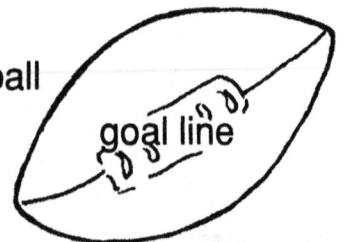

goal line

UNSCRAMBLE THE WORDS TO FIND FIVE OTHER GAMES THAT USE A BALL.

olfg   ginp pnog
ccoers   oellyvabll
tnneis

g _ _ _ _   s _ _ _ _ _ _   t _ _ _ _ _ _
p _ _ _ _ _ _ _   v _ _ _ _ _ _ _ _ _ _

SCORING   38

... IF YOU CONFESS WITH YOUR LIPS THAT "JESUS IS LORD" AND BELIEVE IN YOUR HEART THAT GOD RAISED HIM FROM THE DEAD, YOU WILL BE SAVED.

— ROMANS 10:9

JESUS IS LORD OF OUR HEARTS

JESUS
IS
LORD

selfish
happy
pout
hate
lies
obedience
love for God
gloom
gentle
patience
care
despair
humble
love for others

From the above list find words that describe what you would expect to find in a heart where Jesus is Lord. Write them on the lines in the heart. Can you think of others? Write them in the heart too.

SOME OF THE WORDS IN THE SENTENCES BELOW HAVE MISSING VOWELS. SEE IF YOU CAN COMPLETE THE WORDS WITH a e i o OR u.

If J__s__s is L__rd, we'll l__ve G__d with __ll our h____rts, s____ls and m__nds, and we'll l__ve oth__rs as we l__ve ours__lv__s. We must b__l__eve that J__s__s is truly God's s__n, that he d____d and c__me alive again all for __s to s__ve us from s__n and to s__ve us to a h__ppy l__fe with him n__w and forever.

DRAW A LINE TO THE PIECE THAT MATCHES.

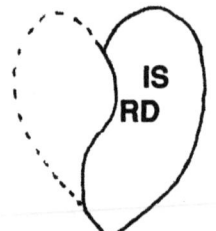

LOVE

IS
RD

JESUS
LO

GOD

LOVE

OTHERS

LOVE GOD

LOVE EACH OTHER

41

ANSWER KEYS

Pages 18, 20, 22

JESUS SAID THIS:

"In everything do to others as you would have them do to you...."
— Matthew 7:12

We call it the **GOLDEN RULE.**

HELP FIND THE BALL.

CROSS OUT THE SENTENCES THAT ARE NOT TRUE.

A game has rules.

~~Each person can make up his or her own rules.~~

We like to win.

A game is ruined if no one plays by the rules.

Jesus gave two great rules or commands.

Life can be ruined if we don't keep the rules Jesus gave.

Jesus' two rules are: love the Lord your God and love your neighbor as yourself.

If we love others, we will do to them what we would like them to do to us.

DRAW A LINE TO THE WORDS THAT FINISH THE SENTENCE. ONE HAS BEEN DONE.

One side — and you're out.
The other side — is behind home plate.
The catcher — love the Lord your God.
The pitcher — runs to first base.
The batter tries — to put the batter out.
Three strikes — is up to bat.
The batter that hits the ball — is in the field.
The fielders try — love your neighbor as yourself.
The batters score — to hit the ball.
The greatest commandment is — throws the ball across home plate.
The second greatest commandment is — if they run the bases safely.

RULES FOR HAPPY LIVING   18

Love the Lord your God with all your heart, and with all your soul, and with all your mind. Love your neighbor as yourself.
—Matthew 22:37, 39

UNSCRAMBLE THE WORDS. THEY ARE ALL FOUND ON THE SCROLL.

oevl	l o v e
roLd	L o r d
lla	l a w
arthe	h e a r t
uols	s o u l
ndim	m i n d
iehgnobr	n e i g h b o r
selfruoy	y o u r s e l f

FILL IN THE SQUARES WITH THE CORRECT WORDS.

L O V E
A
W
S

DOWN
The two rules are called _____.

ACROSS
Jesus' two rules are about _____.

G
O T H E R S
D

DOWN
First we must love _____.

ACROSS
We also must love _____.

FILL IN THE BLANK FROM THE WORD LIST.

Word list: love, washing, eating, scripture, law, days, teaching, prophets, two, drinking

Jesus said the t eaching of the l aw and p rophets of our Old Testament s cripture depends on t wo laws or rules. These are not laws or rules about e ating and d rinking and w ashing or keeping the d ays holy. They are laws about l ove .

IF YOU DO DOT TO DOT IN THE FOUR BOXES, YOU WILL SPELL A WORD.

THE TWO GREATEST COMMANDMENTS: THE LOVE LAWS   20

USE THE CODE IN THE BOX TO FIND ONE OF THE MESSAGES OF JESUS.

1=a	10=n
2=b	11=o
3=d	12=r
4=e	13=s
5=g	14=t
6=h	15=u
7=l	16=v
8=l	17=w
9=m	18=y

v e r y   t r u l y I
16 4 12 18 14 12 15 8 18

t e l l you, a n y o n e who
14 4 8 8   1 10 18 11 10 4

h e a r s my w o r d and
6 4 1 12 13   17 11 12 3

b e l i e v e s him who
2 4 8 4 16 4 13

s e n t me has e t e r n a l life....
13 4 10 14   4 14 4 12 10 1 8

— John 5:24

DO YOU KNOW HOW TO TAKE A MESSAGE FROM SOMEONE ON THE TELEPHONE? IF YOU DON'T KNOW, ASK MOM OR DAD TO TELL YOU.

UNDERLINE THE KIND OF MESSAGE BELOW THAT MIGHT COME ON THE TELEPHONE.

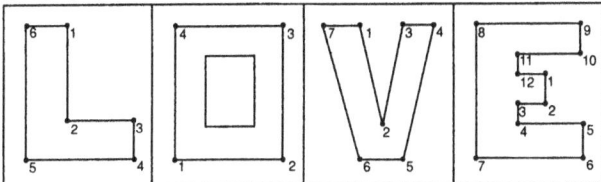

• Dad called to say he'll be late coming home from work.
• Where's my other shoe?
• Grandma called to say they're coming for a visit.
• Bobby hit me.
• Uncle Dan called to say they have a new baby girl.
• Bill called to say he'd pick us up at 9:30 for Sunday school.
• It's not my turn to set the table.
• Mr. Smith called to say he's done with repairs on the bike.
• I don't want to get up yet.

WHERE DO WE FIND THE MESSAGES FROM GOD THAT JESUS BROUGHT TO US? B i b l e

magazines?   dictionary?
map?   telephone directory?
Bible?   newspaper?

COULD A MESSAGE BE IN THE MAILBOX? CAN YOU FIND THE WAY THERE?

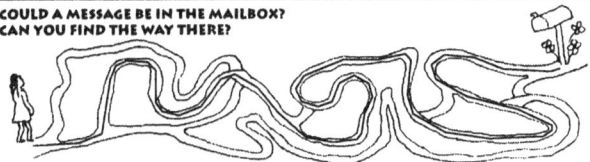

LOVING JESUS, GOD'S MESSENGER   22

ANSWER KEYS

Pages 24, 26, 28

SOME WORDS IN THIS VERSE MIGHT BE HARD TO UNDERSTAND. SEE IF YOU CAN FIGURE OUT THE CORRECT MEANING. DRAW A LINE TO WHAT YOU THINK THE WORD MEANS. WHEN YOU ARE DONE, CHECK YOUR ANSWERS AT THE BOTTOM OF THE PAGE.

Let the word of Christ dwell in you richly; teach and admonish one another in all wisdom; and with gratitude in your hearts sing psalms, hymns, and spiritual songs to God. — Colossians 3:16

1. word of Christ •
2. dwell •
3. richly •
4. teach •
5. admonish •
6. wisdom •
7. psalm •
8. hymns •
9. spiritual •
10. gratitude •
11. hearts •

• 1. place of affections and deep feelings
• 2. thankful for God's goodness
• 3. a sacred song from the Old Testament
• 4. as a precious possession
• 5. understanding what is true and lasting
• 6. live
• 7. gospel
• 8. to help someone learn
• 9. to kindly warn
• 10. a song of praise or joy
• 11. of or about God

CLIMB THE HILL TO CHURCH.

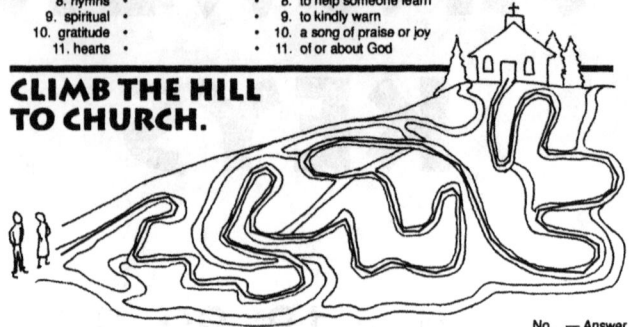

COMPLETE THE VERSE FROM THE WORD LIST BELOW.

FOR WHERE two OR three ARE gathered IN MY name I AM THERE among them.
— MATTHEW 18:20

gathered
I
them
two

among
three
name

LOVING GOD   24

No.	—	Answer
1	—	7
2	—	6
3	—	4
4	—	8
5	—	9
6	—	5
7	—	3
8	—	10
9	—	11
10	—	2
11	—	1

UNSCRAMBLE THE WORDS.
THIS IS MY commandment, THAT YOU love ONE ANOTHER AS I have LOVED you.
— JOHN 15:12

dmtencomman ovle aehv uoy

FIND THE MISSING WORDS TO COMPLETE THE SENTENCE.

Jesus expects his people to love each other.

We must try to obey.

We can love by caring.

We want them to know about Jesus.

We want them to have what they need.

We love others when we pray for them.

vegetables are good for us but we don't love them.

Chocolate chip cookies taste very good but we don't love them.

Love is for God.

Love is for people.

Vegetables
expects
people
taste
Love
pray
obey
Jesus
caring
need

DRAW A LINE TO THE RIGHT VEGETABLE.

Some people put a slice raw on their hamburger.

A slice of this red one is good fresh.

This is good mashed with butter or gravy.

Eat this one cooked and right off the cob.

Cream these for a treat.

These are orange and good in soup.

This one makes good cole slaw.

This one is white with a purple top.

What is it? turnip.

WE ARE GLAD FOR ALL THE GOOD THINGS GOD CREATED FOR US TO ENJOY.

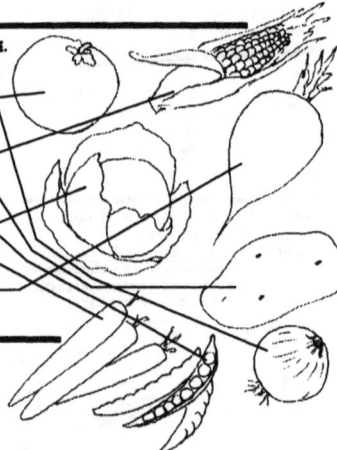

JESUS COMMANDS US TO LOVE   26

FINISH AND COLOR THE bus.

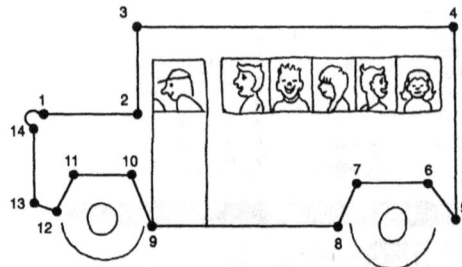

BUSES ARE FOR PEOPLE

A BUS TAKES PEOPLE WHERE THEY NEED TO GO. CHOOSE WORDS FROM THE LIST TO FILL IN THE BOXES AND COMPLETE THE SENTENCE.

People might ride on a bus to
school
or to
grandma's house
or to see a
doctor

England
school
the moon
doctor
fishing
grandma's house

FILL IN THE MISSING LETTERS.

EVERYONE is a Very Important Person!

In Bible times sheep were very valuable. They were used for meat, milk, and clothing. The clothing was either wool or sheep skins. Oil came from sheep, and medicine bottles were made from their horns. A sheep horn was used to call people to worship. Sheep were used in sacrifices as offerings to God. When a poor family only had one, it was usually the family pet. But Jesus said a human being was more valuable than a sheep.

THE NEEDS OF ALL PEOPLE ARE IMPORTANT TO GOD AND TO GOD'S PEOPLE.

I KNOW THAT I AM A VIP BECAUSE JESUS LOVED AND DIED FOR ME.

I KNOW THAT YOU ARE A VIP, TOO, BECAUSE JESUS LOVED AND DIED FOR YOU.

Very Important Person

WE KNOW WHAT'S IMPORTANT   28

ANSWER KEYS

Pages 30, 32, 34

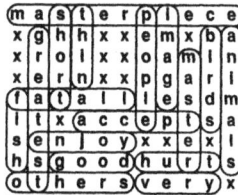

WORDS TO LOOK FOR:

masterpiece	thin	image
greatest	accept	very
others	good	fish
fat	people	birds
tall	master	animals
short	hurt	enjoy

**ALL WORDS GO LEFT TO RIGHT OR DOWN.
CIRCLE THEM AND USE THEM TO FINISH THE SENTENCES BELOW.**

Each of us is a m a s t e r p i e c e made by God the g r e a t e s t old m a s t e r of all. If we think someone is too f a t or t a l l or looks different, remember God made all p e o p l e in his own i m a g e. We a c c e p t everyone the way God has made them, just like we want everyone to accept us. The Bible says God saw all that he had made and it was v e r y g o o d. If we make fun of o t h e r s we h u r t them and we hurt God. God made many masterpieces, f i s h for the sea, b i r d s to fly and all kinds of a n i m a l s. We e n j o y God's wonderful creation.

YOU WILL NEED A PENCIL AND AN ERASER TO DRAW THIS BIRD.

DRAW HERE

1. Draw an oval tipped to one side.
2. Draw a circle on the top end. Draw a long skinny triangle at the other end.
3. Erase the lines as shown.
4. Make a comma shape on the body for the wing. Draw a small triangle on the head for the beak. Make 2 small commas for feet. Add a small circle for the eye.

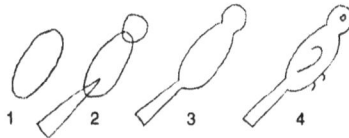

THE GREATEST OLD MASTER   30

PAPER DOLLS IN A CIRCLE

- Use a square piece of paper 8 inches or larger.
- Fold A to B and you have figure 1.
- Fold C to E to get the center line. Undo the fold, figure 1.
- Fold C to D and E to D and you have figure 2.
- Fold along dotted lines shown on figures 3 and 3b.
- Fold K and J backward and you have figure 4.
- Cut along the dotted line L M in figure 5.

There are sixteen layers folded together and each one makes a doll. Draw a doll on the top layer only, figure 6. Cut through all the layers with sharp scissors, figure 7. Do not cut through the ends of the arms or feet, because the dolls are held together at these places.

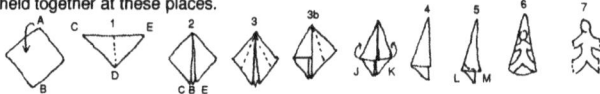

UNSCRAMBLE THE WORDS TO COMPLETE THE BIBLE VERSE.

So then, 1 whenever we have an 2 opportunity, let us 3 work for the 4 good of all, and especially for 5 those of the 6 family of 7 faith. 8 Galatians 6:10

1. enhwvree
2. tunoppityor
3. krwo
4. oodg
5. oesht
6. mlyifa
7. iahtf
8. atGlaains

THERE HAS BEEN A FLOOD. HELP DELIVER WARM BLANKETS.

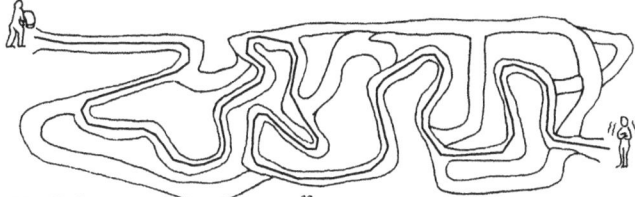

WE INCLUDE ALL   32

FIND THE WORDS YOU NEED TO COMPLETE THE BIBLE VERSES BELOW. THE WORDS GO LEFT TO RIGHT OR DOWN. SEE THE WORD LIST.

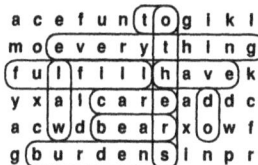

care	others
bear	do
to	fulfill
have	law
everything	burdens

In e v e r y t h i n g do t o o t h e r s what you would h a v e them d o to you.   — Matthew 12:7

B e a r one another's b u r d e n s, and in this way you will f u l f i l l the l a w of Christ.   — Galatians 6:2

One word is left. What is it? c a r e

We ___care___ about how others feel.
(rhymes with bear)

We help ___bear___ their burdens.
(rhymes with care)

LIST SOME WAYS YOU CAN HELP YOUR MOM AND DAD OR PERHAPS YOUR GRANDPARENTS.

_____
_____
_____
_____
_____
_____

DO IS AN ACTION WORD. GOD'S PEOPLE LOOK FOR THINGS THAT NEED DOING.

CARE AND BEAR   34

ANSWER KEYS

Pages 36, 38, 40

UNSCRAMBLE THE WORDS TO MAKE A SENTENCE THAT MOMS AND DADS SAY OFTEN. ouY ustm aresh

You must share.

FILL IN THE BLANKS USING THE RIGHT WORD FROM THE LIST.

God wants us to s h a r e.
When we share we make others h a p p y.
Jesus said it is more blessed to g i v e than to receive.
We make o u r s e l v e s happy when we share.
God wants us to share c h e e r f u l l y.
If we share we are obeying God's r u l e to do to others
as we want them to do to us.

give
happy
ourselves
cheerfully
share
rule

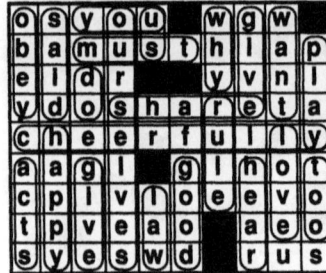

CIRCLE WORDS IN THE BOX THAT ARE IN THE LIST. THE WORDS GO ACROSS TO THE RIGHT OR DOWN.

ACROSS	DOWN	
you	ourselves	obey
must	give (2)	play
share	happy	Acts
cheerfully	rule	hear
	do	why
	love	said
	us	too
	law	want
	good	

READ THE PHRASES. IF THE PHRASE TELLS SOMETHING NICE TO SHARE, DRAW A LINE FROM THE ONE HAS BEEN DONE HOW MANY LINES **PHRASE TO THE SUCKER. TO SHOW YOU HOW. DID YOU DRAW?**

a bad cold
suckers
chickenpox
cookies
a turn on the swing
a piggyback ride with Dad
the front seat of the car

an argument
holding the kitten
a ride in the grocery cart
mud from your feet
batting the ball
crayons
fleas

WHY WE SHARE   36

P e t e r had a question for Jesus.
Peter wanted to know how many times he
should f o r g i v e someone.
Peter thought a S c o r e of seven
times was enough.
Jesus said, "No, not s e v e n times."
Jesus a n s w e r e d, "Forgive
seventy times seven."
Seventy t i m e s seven is 490.

USE THESE WORDS TO COMPLETE THE SENTENCES.

times
seven
forgive
Peter
answered
score

DOWN
Jesus said we must f o r g i v e.

ACROSS
The only way we should keep s c o r e
is in fun.

		f		
s	c	o	r	e
		r		
		g		
		i		
		v		
		e		

WHAT KIND OF BALL IS THIS?

b a s k e t ball

baskets

runs   b a s e ball

Scoring

f o o t ball

goal line

UNSCRAMBLE THE WORDS TO FIND FIVE OTHER GAMES THAT USE A BALL.

olfg   ginp pnog
ccoers   oellyvabll
tnneis

g o l f   s o c c e r   t e n n i s
p i n g p o n g   v o l l e y b a l l

SCORING   38

JESUS IS LORD

obedience
happy
love for others
love for God
patience
gentle
humble
care

selfish
happy
pout
hate
lies
obedience
love for God
gloom
gentle
patience
care
despair
humble
love for others

From the above list find words that describe what you would expect to find in a heart where Jesus is Lord. Write them on the lines in the heart. Can you think of others? Write them in the heart too.

SOME OF THE WORDS IN THE SENTENCES BELOW HAVE MISSING VOWELS. SEE IF YOU CAN COMPLETE THE WORDS WITH a e i o OR u.

If J e s u s is L o rd, we'll l o ve G o d with
a ll our h e a rts, s o u ls and m i nds,
and we'll l o ve oth e rs as we l o ve
ours e lv e s. We must b e l i eve that
J e s u s is truly God's s o n, that he
d i e d and c a me alive again all for u s
to s a ve us from s i n and to s a ve us to
a h a ppy l i fe with him n o w and forever.

JESUS, LORD OF OUR HEARTS   40

DRAW A LINE TO THE PIECE THAT MATCHES.

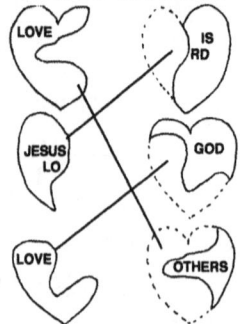

LOVE   IS RD
JESUS LO   GOD
LOVE   OTHERS

www.ingramcontent.com/pod-product-compliance
Lightning Source LLC
Chambersburg PA
CBHW050357100426

42739CB00015BB/3432